Snowflakes Singing Silently

Flurries dance in chilly air,
Like sugar sprinkles everywhere.
They giggle down from skies of gray,
A frosty chorus, come what may.

Chubby flakes in hats and boots,
Twirling gaily, oh what hoots!
They tumble, roll, then softly sigh,
Making snowmen in the sky.

With snowball fights and splashed delight,
They spark a giggle, pure and bright.
Each cold touch is full of cheer,
Warming hearts that gather near.

So catch a flake upon your tongue,
A melting song, forever sung.
In winter's grip, we laugh and play,
As joy's sweet note won't fade away.

Winter's Hidden Delight

In a blanket of white, secrets bloom,
With each snowball, let laughter zoom!
Mittens and hats, all thrown in the air,
Funny faces in frosty flair.

Snowflakes giggle as they race to the ground,
With glee all around, just look at us bound!
Our snowman needs just a pipe and a hat,
Watch him dance in an exaggerated sprawl and spat!

As snow forts rise, great battles begin,
With smiles so wide, who just won the win?
Laughter bubbles in the winter's chill,
With every soft flake, we chase with thrill!

So let us cherish this joyous season,
For in every snowman lies a reason.
To be silly, to play, to sip cocoa's heat,
In winter's delight, life's bitter turns sweet!

A Heart of Snowflakes and Cheer

Gather around, let the stories unfold,
Of snowflakes that tumble, both brave and bold.
With mittens on hands, we cling to the fun,
While hot chocolate melts in the warmth of the sun.

Frosty frolics in the moonlit night,
Sliding down hills, oh what a sight!
With laughter like bells ringing clear,
Every snowman seems to cheer!

Chubby kids with rosy cheeks,
Making angels while the frosty wind speaks.
In a flurry of giggles, we roll and play,
Drawing warmth from the chills of the day.

So embrace the joy as the snowflakes swirl,
Crafting a winter wonder, where laughter will twirl.
With snowmen built, our hearts take flight,
In this fest of fun, everything feels right!

The Joy Within the Frozen World

In winter's grip, we spin and twirl,
Ice cream cones that make us hurl!
With marshmallow hats and silly pranks,
The frozen world gives us silly thanks.

Snowflakes fall with a tickle-light touch,
Each landing softly, oh so much!
With every giggle, the cold feels warm,
As we dance around in our winter charm.

Jokes exchanged by the tabletop trees,
And sipping cocoa with giggles and wheezes.
The frosty air, electric with glee,
In a world so fun, who wouldn't agree?

So raise a mug as the snowflakes shine,
In this frozen land, where laughter is fine.
We toast the joy found in every chill,
As happiness lingers, it's never still!

Chilling Tales Told in Flurries

In the crisp air, laughter dances,
Frosty feet in silly prances.
A carrot nose with a lopsided grin,
Who knew winter could be such a win?

Snowballs flying, a playful fight,
As giggles echo in the fading light.
With each soft landing, a puff of white,
We freeze our hearts, what pure delight!

Snowmen plotting with sticks for hands,
Building dreams in icy strands.
Each block stacked high, a comical sight,
As they join in our frivolous flight!

So here's to fun on winter's stage,
With snowmen grinning, let's engage!
In the frosty chill, we play our part,
With laughter and cheer that warms the heart!

Whimsical Dreams on Snowy Ground

In a world of white where giggles rise,
Snowball battles under clear blue skies.
With hats so big and boots so wide,
We tumble and trip, but we're filled with pride.

The frosty air is filled with cheer,
Each flake that falls brings a new idea.
What if snowmen could really talk?
They'd share their secrets as we walk!

Carrot noses and coal for eyes,
With silly mishaps, they make us rise.
Oh, look at them dance, those frosty pals,
An ice-skating show, oh how it thrills!

As twilight deepens, we gather round,
With cocoa steaming, laughter's loud.
The snowy dreams that fill the air,
Bring joy to hearts, a love we share.

The Enchanted Frost's Embrace

In the morning light, the world's aglow,
With frosty hugs, the chill will flow.
The snowflakes giggle as they start to fall,
Whirling and twirling, they dance for us all.

A snowman prances, his hat askew,
With silly dances, just for a few.
His eyes, they sparkle—oh what a sight!
He's life of the party, laughter ignites!

Candy canes dangle on branches near,
We munch and giggle, spreading good cheer.
The sleigh bells jingle, a magical sound,
While stories of winter swirl all around.

As dusk settles in, we build more fun,
With snowmen lined up, they've just begun.
With joy overflowing, we sing in the cold,
In this frosty realm, we'll never grow old.

Glittering Secrets of the Snowfall

Under the stars, the snowflakes twirl,
Secrets wrapped in a frosty swirl.
"We're magic," they tease, "can you believe?
We make the world sparkle, just to deceive!"

A snowball flies with a playful whack,
Right in the face—there's no turning back!
With laughter ringing, we dash and flee,
A game of tag, wild and free.

The snowman giggles, his buttons jive,
In this wintry world, we feel alive.
He dances 'round with twinkling glee,
A frosty charmer, come join the spree!

As midnight nears, we gather close,
With stories shared, we brag and boast.
The glittering night holds laughter's key,
In every flake, a new joy to see.

Smiles Found in the Frosty Air

A snowy day brings laughter near,
Chasing snowballs, shouting cheer.
With frosty hats and scarves so bright,
We spin and dance in pure delight.

The snowman grins, his nose a carrot,
Did he just wink? Oh, what a ferret!
Around him play the kids so bold,
With giggles flying, tales unfold.

Snowflakes giggle as they land,
Tickling noses, what a plan!
In frosty fields, we jump and twirl,
Who knew cold could be such a whirl?

As evening falls with twinkling lights,
We toast hot cocoa, fables ignite.
With snowman tales, our voices soar,
In laughter's grip, we crave for more.

Frosty Wishes

Frosty fingers disguised as glee,
He whispers dreams of jubilee.
With snowballs flying and laughter loud,
He gathers joy like a fluffy cloud.

His round cheeks puffed with snowy mirth,
Every snowflake claims its worth.
"Hold tight," he shouts, "I'm taking flight!"
Off he goes in frosty delight.

A sleigh ride full of sweet surprise,
Catching snowflakes that kiss the skies.
His laughter echoes, a crisp delight,
Frosty wishes twinkle bright.

Rolling snow in a hastened spree,
Cozy warmth wrapped 'neath a tree.
Brought together by frosty thrills,
A cozy home, where joy fulfills.

The Winter's Delightful Mask

With frosty breath and a jolly face,
He jigs around with snowman grace.
A jaunty step and a playful sway,
He spins and twirls in a snowy ballet.

Wearing socks from Grandma's drawer,
He shuffles around, craving more.
Tickling kids, he breaks the ice,
A frosty prank, oh so nice!

His smile grows as the snowflakes fall,
"What's next?" he shouts, "Do tell, after all!"
Dancing shadows of winter's charm,
He steals the night with his frozen warm.

His cap atop, slightly askew,
Beneath the moonlight, he's quite the view.
So let's all join in, don't be shy,
With a snowman dash, we'll soar and fly!

Luminous Laughter on the Hearth

By the fire, warmth ignites,
Snowflakes tumble in playful flights.
A snowman's grin beams high and wide,
As snowmen tales he won't confide.

Mittens tossed and scarves undone,
He sneezes loudly, oh what fun!
The children giggle and clap with glee,
"Did you see him wink at me?"

His snowy belly bursts with cheer,
A frosty friend who brings good cheer.
With marshmallows dancing atop his hat,
He cracks a laugh, imagine that!

Luminous sights beneath the moon,
In snowy light, he starts to croon.
Belly rolls and joyous sighs,
A festive night 'neath twinkling skies.

The Mirage of a Frosty Grin

In the yard where snowflakes dance,
A frosty face caught in a trance.
Carrot nose and eyes of coal,
Jokes hidden in his snowy soul.

With a hat too big, he tips it wide,
Chasing rabbits that dart and slide.
Laughter echoing from brightened skies,
Mischief glimmers in his eyes.

His belly shakes like a bowl of jelly,
As snowy pals dance, oh so smelly!
Tickling flakes lift his chilly purse,
He howls with giggles, a snowman's verse.

Frosty jokes in a wintry breeze,
Turning frowns into fits of wheeze.
Spreading cheer like frost on trees,
In wonderland, he's sure to tease.

Echoes from the Frostbitten Realm

In frostbitten realms where snowflakes cheer,
The snowman chuckles, spreading good cheer.
With each crisp wind, his laughter flies,
Echoing softly beneath clear skies.

He spins a tale of snowball fights,
Of snow forts built on winter nights.
His giggles rise like frost in the air,
With every joke that he lays bare.

In chilly breaths, the fun ignites,
His frosty cap tilts, oh what sights!
With every step, the ground does squeak,
As laughter echoes, he plays hide and seek.

But as the sun starts to blaze bright,
The jolly fellow takes his flight.
Leaving echoes of joy on the breeze,
In winter's heart, he warms with ease.

Laughter Framed in Crystal Dreams

In crystal dreams where snowflakes gleam,
The snowman plots a silly scheme.
A carrot grin stretched wide as skies,
With candy eyes and laughter flies.

He slides down hills with joyful cheer,
His frosty beard fluffs up like a sphere.
With every bounce, he spins around,
Sending snowballs flying, laughter bound.

He tells of penguins in a band,
Dancing around in perfect stand.
With each snowman sigh, a story starts,
Of winter's fun that warms our hearts.

But when the sun peeks out to play,
His frosty form begins to sway.
In giggles and wiggles, he melts away,
Leaving jokes for the kids to replay.

The Jolly Guardian of Winter's Chill

In a snowy field, he stands so grand,
With a belly laugh like a warm hand.
His scarf flutters like a flag of cheer,
The jolly guardian, we hold dear.

With twiggy arms, he waves to all,
His frosty laugh echoes like a call.
He tells tall tales of winter nights,
Of snowflakes dancing in silly flights.

He roasts marshmallows over cold air,
On frosty lips, giggles to share.
His belly shakes like snow on trees,
A guardian dance in the icy breeze.

But when he trips on his own foot,
The whole world bursts with giggles, whoot!
As snowflakes tumble all around,
Laughter fills the frosty ground.

Frozen Secrets Beneath the Frost

Beneath cold layers, secrets hide,
There's a carrot nose and eyes of pride.
But when it melts, oh what a tale,
The snowman's jokes begin to pale.

With frosty breath and silly stance,
He moonwalks in a snowy dance.
A snowball fight with no snowballs,
Just fluffy flakes as laughter calls.

A friendly wave with frosted hands,
He juggles snowflakes, making plans.
But lose a hat and gain a chill,
That frosty grin will haunt you still.

As winter fades, the fun runs dry,
The snowman winks, his time to fly.
With frozen secrets in the air,
He leaves behind a chilly stare.

Frozen Smiles

A jolly fellow made of white,
With sparkling eyes that shine so bright.
He points his stick to silly sights,
And spins around in frosty nights.

With snowflakes landing on his head,
He giggles softly in his bed.
His mouth a curve of pure delight,
Reflects the joy of winter's height.

He shares a joke with passing birds,
That flit and chirp with silly words.
They laugh together, a frosty cheer,
In the magic of the winter sphere.

So if you see him on your way,
Join the fun and dance and play.
For frozen smiles and joyful glee,
Make winter bright for you and me.

Echoes in the Winter

The chill of winter sings a tune,
Of frosty pranks 'neath silvery moon.
With giggles echoing down the lanes,
The snowman grins as joy he gains.

Each snowflake dances in delight,
As he recounts his funny plight.
With a hat too big and scarf so bright,
He craves the warmth of laughter's light.

He tells a tale of snowball kings,
And all the slide and silly things.
The cheerful shouts and playful calls,
Ring out among the snowy walls.

So when you hear the winter's cheer,
Remember the grin that draws you near.
For laughter dwells where snowflakes play,
In frozen echoes of the day.

The Snowy Grin

A frosty smile that beams so wide,
With every blizzard, he takes pride.
His cheeks are red from cold and cheer,
While all around, the world draws near.

He holds a twig with playful flair,
And dances in the wintry air.
With a flip and twist, he spins around,
As snowy laughter fills the ground.

His snowball stash, a playful sight,
Caught by surprise in mid-flight.
A giddy spark in every throw,
A friend to share the winter glow.

So if you meet his playful grin,
Just join the fun and jump right in!
For in the frosty, gleeful rhyme,
Lies laughter waiting every time.

Secrets Beneath the Frost

Underneath the snowy cap,
A carrot nose will take a nap.
With coal eyes that laugh and stare,
He winks at snowflakes in the air.

His frosty hat holds tales so bright,
Of snowball fights that last all night.
A friend to rabbits, sly and spry,
He tells them jokes as they hop by.

Mittens tucked within his chest,
He holds the secrets of the rest.
With every flake that tumbles down,
He chuckles softly, wearing frowns.

A snowman's joy is pure delight,
In every drift and soft moonlight.
For in his heart, he hides away,
The giggles of a snowy day.

The Joyful Shadow of a Winter's Day

Under the sun, he casts a grin,
With twinkling eyes, a frosty din.
He tells a joke, it's quite absurd,
The crack of laughter, such a herd!

Frosty friends in snowball fights,
With snowflakes dancing, pure delights.
Their laughter echoes, fills the air,
While snowmen wink with cheeky flair.

He found a hat, a funny dress,
In winter's charm, there's fun, no less.
A joyful heart, a chilly day,
With snowy magic, come what may.

Laughter Painted in White

Snowflakes shower, a fluffy dream,
Yet here comes Frosty with a gleam.
His silly grin a sight to see,
He dances wild, so carefree.

With mittens on, he runs amok,
Tripping over a frozen rock.
The kids all chuckle and shout with glee,
As he spins round, a clumsy spree.

Hot cocoa waits, a warm embrace,
But first, he must win the snowy race.
He dives right in, a belly flop,
With giggles bubbling, they can't stop.

A Frosty Wreath of Delight

The breeze brings giggles, frosty cheer,
As snowflakes tickle every ear.
A wreath of dreams hangs on the door,
With jingle bells that clink and score.

Plump snowmen stand with glee so wide,
Each carrot nose a silly guide.
With scarves so bright, they strut and pose,
As laughter spills from furry toes.

Snowball fights erupt with glee,
As playful spirits roam so free.
In icicle castles, fun abounds,
Where frosty joy in laughter grounds.

Hushed Happiness Beneath the Flurry

A jolly figure stands so bright,
With buttons of coal, what a sight!
He trips on ice, oh what a fall,
His hat flies high, a snowy ball.

Children giggle in delight,
As carrots dance in morning light.
His nose is crooked, laughs ensue,
He gives a wave, what else to do?

Snowflakes land and twirl around,
His laughter echoes, quite profound.
With fluffy arms, he starts to sway,
Chasing snowballs on display.

Secrets of Winter's Heart

In the quiet of night, he shares a tale,
Of snowball fights and winter gales.
Snowman secrets, shared with glee,
Frosty giggles beneath the tree.

With every flake that tickles his cheek,
He chuckles softly, so unique.
A shivery chuckle, a chilly cheer,
Winter's heart laughs, while friends draw near.

Grinning Against the Cold

He cheekily rolls in a snowman ball,
Grinning wide, he's having a ball.
Snowflakes fall, he does a jig,
Happy and plump, a snowman gig.

Frosty fun beneath the moonlight,
His laugh echoes, pure delight.
Against the cold, he stands so proud,
A beacon of joy, singing loud.

Frosted Delight

With buttons straight from Grandma's stash,
He dances in snow with a lively splash.
Twinkling eyes, so bright and bold,
Frosted delight, a story unfolds.

Sliding on ice, he takes a spill,
Giggles surround him, oh what a thrill!
A top hat perched, a crooked style,
Chasing the chill with a frosty smile.

Joy Encased in Ice

A frosty grin, all aglow,
With a carrot nose, here we go!
He juggles snowballs, oh what a sight,
Spreading giggles, pure delight.

In a cozy scarf, he takes a bow,
Winking at friends with snow on his brow.
Snowflakes tickle, laughter takes flight,
Joy encased in ice, a heart so light.

Frosted Tales of Cheer

In snow-covered fields, laughter grows,
Tales of frost and jolly shows.
Snowball fights, a fluffy spree,
Frosty fun beneath the tree.

Watch them trip and make a scene,
Smiling wide with faces clean.
Silly jokes in winter's light,
Snowman grins shining bright.

Rolling snowballs, hands so cold,
With stories of cheer still being told.
In frozen lands, the spirits play,
Frosted adventures on display.

Laughter echoes, hearts so bold,
Through winter's chill, the warmth unfolds.
With every snowflake, a friendly cheer,
In the frosty air, joy draws near.

The Jolly Spirit in White

In a garden dressed in white,
Snowmen gather, a merry sight.
With silly hats and scarves so bright,
They celebrate the chilly night.

A jolly chorus, songs take flight,
Hopping around, pure delight.
Snow-covered cheeks and jests abound,
Echoes of cheer in frosty ground.

Riding on sleds, they zoom so fast,
In winter's dance, joy holds steadfast.
Tripping and tumbling, laughter spills,
Frosty mischief gives heart thrills.

With every snowflake falling down,
Giggles rise up in vibrant town.
In icy hugs, the warmth ignites,
With frozen fun, the spirit delights.

Grins Amidst the Chill

A snowman's grin, oh what a tease,
Wobbling 'round in the winter breeze.
With button eyes that wink and blink,
He's up to mischief, what do you think?

Frosty friends on sleds so bright,
Zooming past in pure delight.
Snowballs fly like little dreams,
In the snowy world, laughter beams.

Their noses poked at every turn,
Making snow angels, watch them learn.
With frosty limbs and chilly toes,
Laughter bubbles where the cold wind blows.

A snowy dance, a silly show,
In frigid air, their giggles grow.
Chasing snowflakes, they take a leap,
In a winter's whirl, the joy runs deep.

The Laughter of Frozen Days

In a field of white, they play,
Little snowballs jump and sway.
A carrot nose with a funny twist,
Chasing shadows, none can resist.

Snowflakes tickle, laughter rings,
Snowmen dance and do silly things.
A flurry of giggles fills the air,
Frozen friends without a care.

Sleds and slips, they tumble down,
Frosty puns in winter's crown.
With frosty hats all askew,
In the sun's glow, smiles break through.

In the chill, warm hearts ignite,
Giggles blazing, oh what a sight!
With icy grins, they cheerfully frown,
The laughter echoes through the town.

Enigmas of the Winter Gale

Fluffy flakes whirl, he spins around,
Chuckling softly at the silence found.
He pulls a snow cat out from his hat,
With a flick of his wrist, imagine that!

Under starlit skies, he shares a grin,
With fun-filled tales that dance in the wind.
Winter's mystery, wrapped in delight,
As he creates joy, on a frosty night.

Cheery Shadows of the Snow

His shadow dances, a jolly chap,
While squirrels gather for a winter nap.
With a twirl of snow, he starts to tease,
As icicles dangle from frozen trees.

A snowball fight, he can't resist,
Waging a war, with a frosty fist.
The laughter echoes through winter's chill,
As the snowman grins, he's king of the hill.

Winter's Silent Amusement

In a snowy park, he takes a stance,
With a goofy grin, ready to prance.
The children giggle, toss snowballs high,
He dodges them all, oh what a guy!

With boots made of laughter, he trudges along,
Singing to snowflakes, a comical song.
His frosty tricks, a playful delight,
In the moonlit magic of the snowy night.

The Glow in Winter's Heart

A carrot nose so bright and bold,
He tells a joke that never gets old.
With coal for eyes that twinkle and gleam,
He dances in snow, living the dream.

Snowflakes chuckle, fall from the sky,
As he tips his hat, oh my, oh my!
His scarf flutters with a gleeful flair,
Winter's laughter fills the frosty air.

Chilling Laughter

In a frozen field where the chill kicks in,
Snowmen gather, wide smiles, it's a win.
As gales of laughter fill the air,
Their comical antics draw everyone near.

Rolling in snow, they tumble and cheer,
Building tall towers, feeling no fear.
With flurries of snowballs, they aim for the best,
But end up giggling—each one a jest!

With a dance and a spin, oh what a sight,
Their frosty bodies twinkle in the night.
Each jolly chuckle is music anew,
In the land of the frosted, where fun's never few.

So hats off to winters, and laughter's delight,
In a world filled with smiles, every chill feels right.
With every snowflake that drifts from the sky,
We celebrate fun with a twinkle and sigh.

Frosted Dreams

In a winter wonderland brimming with cheer,
Frosty figures graze on snowflakes near.
With grins like sunshine, they share their schemes,
Crafting frosted delights from dreams.

They build a fort, a snowman brigade,
With top hats perched, they're never afraid.
Snowballs fly in comical arcs,
Laughter erupting like joyful sparks.

Sipping on cocoa, they trade silly tales,
Of frosty adventures and whimsical trails.
With every sip, a chuckle escapes,
Amidst snowy peaks and frosty drapes.

As night falls down, the stars align,
These merry beings, so full of shine.
With magic alive, their grins spread wide,
In the frosted dreams where laughter won't hide.

Frost-kissed Whimsies Under the Stars.

Beneath the moon, the snowmen prance,
Twinkling lights give them a chance.
With frosty hats and scarves so bright,
They waltz together, a comical sight.

While children snooze in a cozy bed,
The snowmen dance on with laughter widespread.
A snowball missed can spark a delight,
As they tumble down, all giggles and fright.

With arms of sticks and a cheeky grin,
They slide down hills, eager to win.
In every snowdrift, a new game unfolds,
Where the tales of snowmen and laughter are told.

So if you peek out while the stars glow,
You might catch the fun of this frosty show.
With every sparkle and chortle they'd bring,
A light-hearted joy that makes the heart sing.

Magic of the Snow-Covered Smirk

In a snowy coat, so round and bright,
A jolly smile sparkles in the night.
With a carrot nose and eyes like coal,
He dances on ice, a merry soul.

Snowflakes swirl, a frosty delight,
His happy grin glows with pure light.
Twirling in circles, he skips with glee,
Chasing the children, wild and free.

Mid snowball fights, he can't hold a frown,
Each playful hit, he topples down.
With laughter echoing through the air,
His goofy jig—no one can compare!

And when the sun melts away his cheer,
He leaves behind joy for all to hear.
In every flake that falls from above,
Lies a tale of frost and playful love.

Happy Chills of December

In December's embrace, where giggles reside,
A snowman capers with no need to hide.
With mittens so bright and his cheeks all aglow,
He twirls through the wonder, a jolly show.

Snowballs are flying, it's a frosty delight,
Each toss brings a giggle under the moonlight.
His grin broadens wider as friends gather near,
In the heart of the chill, there's nothing to fear.

The Jester of the Snowfeld

In the frosty field, he jigs and he prances,
With a belly that shakes, as he takes his chances.
A snowman comedian, with a laugh so loud,
He draws in a crowd and makes them so proud.

His scarf flaps wildly in the icy breeze,
Telling snow tales that bring all to their knees.
With a wink and a grin, he cheers up the skies,
For laughter is sunshine, the cold can't disguise.

Glances of Icy Joy

With a twirl and a spin, he catches a drift,
His playful antics are the season's gift.
Children all laugh as they toss snowy balls,
Creating a ruckus in the winter's sprawls.

His frosty smirk shines, making all hearts sing,
As snowflakes dance around like they're on a swing.
Each little giggle floats into the air,
A sprinkle of joy that's beyond compare.

The Playful Chill

A frosty fellow with a button nose,
Wobbles and giggles as the cold wind blows.
His hat's a little crooked, a comical sight,
Dancing with snowflakes under the moonlight.

He rolls in the snow with a big jolly snort,
Building a snow fort, a snowy resort.
With carrots for eyes, and a smile so wide,
He piles up the snow, full of playful pride.

The Frost-Kissed Grin

Under the stars, his smile beams,
In the chilly night, full of dreams.
With a wink, he starts to sway,
Bringing laughter into play.

A snowflake tickles on your nose,
The frosty fun just grows and grows.
Tumbling down in this delight,
A playful chase, what a sight!

Frosty dance in moonlight glow,
A joyful echo in the snow.
The grin so wide, you can't resist,
In winter's charm, we must persist.

Winter's Embrace

Snowflakes flutter, soft and light,
Children laugh, what a sight!
With each toss, a glittery flair,
Winter magic fills the air.

Frosty friends with frolicsome hearts,
Sliding down, their glee imparts.
Snowmen chuckle, and so they play,
In the chilly, bright ballet.

A snowball here, a snowman there,
Creating chaos everywhere.
In this wonder, so much fun,
Sprinkled joy, the day's begun.

Frost's Cheery Countenance

A snowy face with eyes so bright,
Winks at you in pure delight.
He starts a snowball fight with glee,
Frosty fun for you and me.

Each flake that falls is a silly tease,
Twirling down from frosty trees.
A winter dance, a merry sound,
Laughter echoes all around.

Jolly grins and silly slips,
Hot cocoa warms our frozen lips.
With every tumble and every roll,
The snowman's joy just fills the soul.

Enchanted Snowplay

In the frosty field they flop,
Snowballs fly, a winter pop.
Giggling kids, a joyful base,
Building smiles in every space.

Carrot noses, a laugh so wide,
With floppy hats, they take a ride.
Snowflakes dance around their feet,
Magic moments, oh so sweet.

Chilly cheeks, a rosy glow,
Frosty frolics, high and low.
Sledding down the hills so steep,
In snow's embrace, they leap and creep.

The Smile of Icicles

Icicles dangle, like teeth made of glass,
The snowman chuckles at the flakes as they pass,
His cheeks rosy red, with a mischievous spark,
Creating a ruckus in the frost-laden park!

He pulls funny faces, in frost he is clad,
Tickling the ice with a joke never bad,
His laughter rings clear, like a bell's merry chime,
In the wintery wonder, he captures the rhyme.

Embrace in the Snowfall

Beneath the soft glow of a cold winter's light,
The snowman embraces the frosty delight,
With arms made of branches, reaching so wide,
He welcomes the giggles; come play by his side!

His hat is askew, but his spirit is bright,
A companion to all in the shimmering night,
With snowballs a-flying and laughter on deck,
He spins round and round — oh, what a wreck!

Playful Winter Whimsy

Snowflakes giggle as they tumble and glide,
The chubby snowman laughs with ebullient pride,
His hat's slightly crooked, his scarf's in a knot,
Oh, what a sight, quite the whimsical plot!

He juggles the snowballs, oh what a show,
They bounce off his belly, they tumble and go,
With each little blunder, the kids shout with glee,
A slippery dance with a flair, can you see?

Shadows of Laughter

In a coat of white, he prances and twirls,
With buttons of coal and a grin that whirls,
His carrot nose wiggles, a jolly old chap,
As snowflakes dance down with a playful clap.

He tells snowball jokes, oh, aren't they a hit?
Frosty puns fly as he tickles and sits,
Under the moon, he gleefully sways,
In the cold, frosty air, he merrily plays.

Glimmers in the Chill

In the icy light, giggles float by,
With sparkles that shimmer like candy in the sky.
A snowman with charm, and a laugh that's a cheer,
Turns every cold moment into joyful sphere.

His nose gives a wiggle, as snowflakes applaud,
While snowball fights erupt, almost like a plod.
With a hop and a skip, he dances abroad,
Creating a winter wonder, a fun-loving facade.

The Merry Ice Guardian

The guardian of ice, with jokes up his sleeve,
Telling tales of snow and how to believe.
He pranks with the frost, and all join the fun,
While snowflakes chuckle, one by one.

With twig arms outstretched, he dances in place,
A merry old figure with a silly old face.
Sliding down hills, in a flurry of grace,
For winter's a party, and he's in the race.

Gentle Breath of Snow

A soft breath of winter, laughter in tow,
Little mittens warm hands, as children glow.
A snowman with style, wearing shades and a hat,
Who knew that snow could be such a brat?

With a belly so round, he rolls in delight,
Spinning around, giving snowballs a fright.
Each tumble and giggle, a magical sight,
As wintertime frolics turn day into night.

Mirth of the Winter Spirit

In the frosty air, giggles arise,
Snowflakes dance down, like fuzzy butterflies.
The snowman grins, with a carrot nose,
Spreading cheer like it's the best winter prose.

His button eyes twinkle, mischief in sight,
While kids throw snowballs, their laughter takes flight.
One cheeky snowman, with a scarf so bright,
Winks at the world, bringing pure delight.

Laughter in the Flurries

As flurries dance, he strikes a pose,
With arms outstretched, he strikes a doze.
With every gust of chilly air,
His frosty antics, unaware.

Kids gather round to join the fun,
In snowball fights, they'll run and run.
His laughter echoes through the trees,
An icy friend, with every breeze.

Twirling flakes, and muffled cheers,
He jests with snowmen hiding near.
Beneath the moonlit, glimm'ring stare,
Each snowy smile, a joyful flair.

When winter's grip begins to fade,
His chuckles linger, memories made.
A snowman's charm, a sight so grand,
In every heart, warmth walks hand in hand.

The Hidden Joy of Winter's Glow

The sunbeam tickles frosty trees,
While ice bubbles dance with ease.
Little critters join the spree,
In cozy nooks, all filled with glee.

Bundled hats and scarves galore,
Slip and slide on snowy floor.
Giggles echo through the chill,
As snowflakes twirl with raucous thrill.

In whispers soft and playful grace,
The playful winds know every face.
Winter's glow brings warmth inside,
With laughter that we cannot hide.

So take a chance, let laughter flow,
Feel the spark of winter's glow.
In every flake, a giggle found,
Joyful echoes all around.

Frosted Laughter on a Winter's Night

As night falls down in purest white,
Silly shadows come to light.
Snowmen prance in moon's soft beam,
With carrot noses, what a dream!

Chortling breezes spin the air,
Twinkling stars join in the flair.
Marshmallow clouds drift with a grin,
While frosty sprites spin into sin.

With each ice-crunching joyful sound,
Holiday cheer is all around.
Giggles burst like popcorn pop,
Under the starlit winter's top.

A snowy scene with frosted cheer,
In every laugh, there's love held dear.
As winter sleeps in peaceful plight,
Together we bask in the night.

A Sledding Serenade to the Stars

Down the hill, we swoosh and glide,
With cheeks aglow and hearts wide.
Sleds like rockets, zooming past,
A winter joy that's unsurpassed.

Laughter echoes crisp and bright,
As snowflakes twirl in pure delight.
Each thrilling ride inspires a cheer,
The cold can't touch our warmth right here.

With every bump and joyful shout,
We navigate the snowy route.
Powerful winds may push and sway,
But we find fun in every play.

Under starlit skies so vast,
In winter's arms, we drift so fast.
A sledding serenade, we sing,
To nature's winter, joy we bring.

Frosty Comraderie

In winter's chill, they gather round,
With carrot noses, laughter found.
Snowballs fly, a cheeky throw,
Each icy prank steals the show.

With top hats perched, they share a jest,
In snowy realms, they are the best.
Rolling in fluff, they gleefully churn,
Chasing each other, no time to spurn.

Around the fire, stories spin,
Of frosty feats that lead to grins.
They tip their hats, a hearty cheer,
As snowflakes dance, there's joy to hear.

These jolly pals, with rosy cheeks,
Finding fun in frozen peaks.
With every laugh, they shine so bright,
Turning cold days into delight.

The Laughter of Snowflakes

Snowflakes tumble, a playful race,
Twisting and turning in frosty space.
They giggle as they flutter down,
Draping the world in a silvery gown.

Frosty friends join in the spree,
Creating chaos with glee,
A snowy dance, a swirl and spin,
In the chill, their joy begins.

Catch them on tongues, a sweet surprise,
Each flake a jester in the skies.
Laughter echoes through the trees,
As winter playmates tease and please.

In this landscape, laughter reigns,
With frozen humor in their veins.
Through the flurries, their giggles soar,
A symphony of fun forevermore.

Enigmatic Winter Wonders

Amidst the frost, strange wonders gleam,
A snowman's hat hides secrets, it seems.
With buttons sewn in a random style,
He cracks a grin, then breaks into smile.

Tracks in the snow lead to a riddle,
Why did the snowman start to skittle?
With arms outstretched, he prances about,
In the winter's game, there's no room for doubt.

Mystic snowflakes with tales to tell,
Each one whispers a whimsical spell.
Through icy realms, they twirl and frolic,
Making magic, oh so nostalgic!

In the stillness of night, they twinkle bright,
Creating mischief under the moonlight.
New snowmen arise, having fun,
As laughter and joy have only begun.

Smiles Beneath a Blanket of Snow

Beneath drifts deep, laughter peeks,
As winter winks and softly speaks.
Snowmen gather, arms open wide,
In snowball fights, they take great pride.

With every plop of snow on the ground,
Joyous giggles are lost and found.
They wiggle and wobble in playful tune,
Reveling 'neath the bright, snowy moon.

Snowflakes tumble like tiny clowns,
In a world where frowns turn upside downs.
With scarves that flutter like flamboyant flags,
These frosty pals dance without drags.

As winter spreads her icy sheet,
The joy of the season can't be beat.
In frosty air, the laughter flows,
With shivers of fun beneath white throes.

The Glee Beneath the Icicles

In the chill of the frosty air,
A snowman grins without a care.
His carrot nose, a curious sight,
Winks at snowflakes in cozy flight.

Children giggle, snowballs fly,
As he dances, no need to try.
With a twirl and a silly jig,
He pops a snow hat, oh so big!

Icicles hang like silly teeth,
While snowmen prank with winter's wreath.
They play tricks on those who pass,
Their laughter echoes like soft glass.

Underneath the bright winter moon,
Snowmen hum a merry tune.
With frozen arms raised up high,
A joyful dance 'neath the sky.

The Cheerful Chill

Frosty fingers in the breeze,
Tickle noses, oh what a tease!
With each snowflake's playful dive,
The winter world feels so alive!

Snowman rolls with carefree cheer,
Embracing snowballs tossed near.
He juggles them like snowy eggs,
While kids laugh and dance on legs.

Sledding down a hill so steep,
He's right there, with a snowball heap.
A playful toss, a little slip,
And down he goes on a snowdrift trip!

With a frosty grin on his face,
He spins around at a lively pace.
Winter giggles all around,
As joy and snowflakes swirl and bound.

The Frosted Charm of Winter

In a snowy world, so bright and white,
Snowmen bloom with pure delight.
Each snowball they toss with glee,
Becomes a moment, wild and free.

With hats askew and scarves that fly,
They dance beneath the cobalt sky.
Frosty friends, a playful bunch,
Laughing hard, they share a crunch.

Sparkling eyes and smiles wide,
Each snowman holds a secret side.
With snowflake magic in their spark,
They twirl and jive in the dreamy park.

A snowman's charm, oh what a vibe!
With dancing joy, they come alive.
Winter's fun like a playful spark,
Painting laughter in the park.

Radiance of a Snowy Grin

Round and round, the snowflakes swirl,
Snowmen giggle as they twirl.
Their arms wide open, they embrace the drift,
As kids cheer on, giving them a lift!

A carrot nose and a scarf that flies,
With sparkle in their mittened eyes.
Sleds and snowmen race on by,
With every turn, they reach for the sky!

Frosty friends on winter days,
Pickle faces, oh what a craze!
Every snowball holds laughter inside,
In winter's magic, joy does abide.

As the sun sets, a warm glow spins,
Snowmen bask with cheeky grins.
In the dance of snowflakes' gleam,
They spin and prance in a frosty dream.

Cheer Encased in Icicles

With a carrot nose, he stands so spry,
Wobbling with joy, hand-knit bowtie.
His eyes made of coal, they gleam with glee,
Sipping hot cocoa, he's as merry as can be.

In his frosty hat, a secret he keeps,
Snowflakes dance around as he giggles and leaps.
Built by kids who've thrown snowball fights,
He chuckles along through long winter nights.

Each flake that falls, he catches with cheer,
"Snow much fun!" he yells, "Let's build another, dear!"
Sprinkling laughter in the frosty air,
A jolly old frosty, without any care.

So if you find him, give a hearty wave,
For his cheerful spirit, we all want to save.
This jester of winter, with icicles of grace,
Brings a jolly library of smiles to the place.

Glistening Mirth on a Winter's Breath

Under a moon that's twinkling bright,
A snowman dances in the soft starlight.
His carrot dance moves are truly bizarre,
While he dreams of hot cocoa in a snowy bazaar.

With buttons of glass and a scarf of red,
He spins and twirls, losing his head.
The chill tickles his frosty toes,
As he treks through the snow, where nobody goes.

A playful wink, with a cheeky grin,
He holds snowball fights like he's born to win.
Nearby snowflakes hear him chant and cheer,
"Let's throw some snow, it's the best time of year!"

So grab your mittens, it's time to play,
Join the snowman on his frosty ballet.
With laughter that sparkles, like snow in the sun,
You'll find winter magic - it's all about fun!

Smiles Crafted from Winter's Breath

With a belly that shakes like a bowl full of snow,
He tells silly jokes; he's the star of the show.
"Knock, knock!" he calls, with a belly laugh,
"Who's there?" we answer, "Frosty the gaff!"

Chasing his hat, he zooms like a bird,
Fumbling for mittens, he's truly absurd.
He shimmies and slides down the hill with a shriek,
Leaving snowmen giggling, so merry, so sleek.

Around him, kids laugh, as snowballs fly,
His smile a beacon under the cloudy sky.
"I'm not just made of snow, I'm humor and cheer!"
His joyous laughter echoes far and near.

So come join the fun, don't you dare hesitate,
With this frosty friend, let's celebrate.
Smiles crafted from fluffy winter surprise,
He's the snowman of joy, joyful and wise!

The Playful Heart of December

In December's heart, where the snowflakes play,
A cheeky snowman grins, come join the fray.
With branches for arms and a grin oh so wide,
He leaps and he bounds, a wintertime guide.

Making snow angels and sliding on ice,
He jokes and he prances, "This weather's so nice!"
"Hurry, throw snow, let's build and create,
Funny little snow forts, oh isn't this great?"

When the moon shines bright, he'll host a grand ball,
With snowflakes as fairies dancing for all.
He teaches us laughter, the joy of delight,
"Frosty fun times make this world feel so bright!"

So as days grow colder, and the world turns to white,
Remember the snowman, spreading mirth in the night.
The playful heart of December hears the sound,
Of giggles and joy in the snow-covered ground.

Chilled Whispers of Delight

In the yard, a snowman stands tall,
With a carrot nose, he welcomes all.
His button eyes twinkle, mischief in sight,
Spreading giggles from morning to night.

Children gather, their laughter rings,
Snowballs fly as winter sings.
A scarf that's too big, it sways with cheer,
Our frosty friend knows no fear.

With arms made of branches, he dances with glee,
Belly laughs echo, like a winter spree.
His frosty grin tells a cozy tale,
Of snowball fights that never grow stale.

As the sun shines bright, he starts to melt,
Yet his humor lingers, warmth truly felt.
A puddle of joy, where he used to stand,
Leaves memories of fun, life's winter band.

Frosty Mirth

In a world where snowflakes twirl and spin,
A jolly snowman wears a great big grin.
With a top hat crooked, and sticks for arms,
He charms the children with his silly charms.

The sun peeks out, and he starts to sway,
Dancing to tunes from a snow-filled ballet.
His laughter rings, a sound so bright,
Frosty giggles, pure delight.

Snowballs tumble, and snowflakes glide,
Behind his frosty coat, there's nothing to hide.
With a twirl and a spin, he gives a shout,
"Let's play together! Come on, don't pout!"

As icicles gleam, he gives a wink,
"More fun to be had, don't forget to think!"
In the winter wonderland, he's our guide,
With frosty mirth, there's nothing to bide.

The Icon of Icy Happiness

A snowman stands where the cold winds blow,
His belly round, and his joy on show.
With candy cane arms, he waves to the crowd,
A beacon of laughter, merry and loud.

Children clamor, "Let's build him a hat!"
A wonky creation – a pink fluffy cat!
His eyes made of coal, they sparkle and gleam,
An icon of fun, living the dream.

Through the chilly air, he starts to glide,
With a belly flop, he joins in with pride.
Rolling in snow, he gives a big cheer,
"A winter of giggles, now that I'm here!"

As the snowflakes twirl, he jests with flair,
His frosty persona spreads joy everywhere.
With each passing moment, he warms up the day,
An icon of happiness, come out and play!

Winter's Daring Smile

Beneath the bright sun, he stands so stout,
With a truely daring smile, there's no doubt.
Snowflakes shimmer as they fall around,
In his frosty magic, laughter is found.

A playful wink and a jiggle of snow,
His funny antics steal the whole show.
With a sledding spree down the icy hill,
He giggles and tumbles, what a wild thrill!

Snowman's delight, kids jumping with joy,
He's the center of fun, a winter toy.
With a belly of snow and a heart of cheer,
He brings all the kids, from far and near.

As day turns to dusk, he waves goodnight,
His daring smile fades, but spirits stay bright.
Though winter will pass, memories hold tight,
To the laughter and fun in the soft moonlight.

The Heart of Winter's Merriment

In a scarf too tight, he makes a scene,
With buttons that jolt, and a hat so keen.
He stumbles and giggles, a frosty delight,
Chasing little snowflakes, oh what a sight!

His carrot nose wiggles, while children cheer,
He dances on ice, with no hint of fear.
With a belly like jelly, he rolls down the hill,
In laughter and joy, his heart loves to thrill!

A mitten on one hand, a broom in the other,
He twirls like a dancer, my frosty old brother.
With each silly fall, and each clumsy spin,
He brings out the giggles, from deep within!

When the sun starts to shine, he starts to drift,
But in our hearts forever, he gifts us his gift.
So let's raise a cup, to this jolly old chap,
For winter's not winter, without his wild lap!

Icy Tales of Glee

On a bright winter's morning, he strikes quite a pose,
With a smile so big, that it tickles your toes.
He juggles some snowballs, a slippery game,
And just when you watch, he gets hit and he's lame!

He rolls in the snow, making snow angels wide,
Then slips on a patch, and slides like a glide.
Oh how the kids laugh, as he skids all around,
A frosty old fellow, who's silliness found!

With snowflakes a-flying, he spins with wild flair,
Creating a snowstorm that tickles the air.
With a wink and a grin, he tiptoes with sass,
Then flops on his back, hoping none see him pass!

As the daylight fades, and the night softly glows,
He shares frosty tales about his wintery woes.
A giggle, a chuckle, a whimsical tune,
With frosty adventures beneath the bright moon!

The Joy Beneath the Shimmer

As the snowflakes fall down, he begins to jiggle,
With a frosty old grin, he dances and giggles.
His cheeks rosy red, from the cold winter chill,
With every small bounce, he exudes such a thrill!

He builds a tall tower out of white fluffy fluff,
But just when it's done, the wind plays it rough.
Down crashes the snowman, with hardly a fuss,
And up bursts the laughter—oh, winter's a must!

With hot cocoa sips, he tells tales of cheer,
About snowy adventures that bring everyone near.
A hop, skip, and jump with a laugh in the air,
Together they play, without a single care!

When the moon starts to rise, and stars start to gleam,
He waves at the children—in their dreams, they all beam.
A night full of chatter, and dreams spread so wide,
With echoes of laughter where happiness hides!

Secrets of the Frosty Facade

Behind the chilly grin, there's a secret that's bright,
A heart full of laughter, that shines through the night.
With snowflakes that tickle and twirl all around,
He jests like a clown, with joy that is found!

A floppy old hat perched a bit askew,
He waves to the dogs, and the kids playing too.
In the hush of the dusk, he pulls off a prank,
With a dance on the ice, oh, my frosty old prank!

He gathers up snow for a snowball fight,
With a chuckle and cheer, he takes off in flight.
But when he gets hit, oh, the laughter erupts,
His belly rolls so pretty, as he bounces and supes!

As the winter winds slow, and the twilight descends,
He gathers up stories, from playful amends.
So here's to the laughter, the joy that ensues,
In the heart of the cold, we find warmth in our views!

Milton Keynes UK
Ingram Content Group UK Ltd.
UKHW021951151124
451186UK00007B/188

9 789916 943908